SUPER
BIKES

Series creator:

David Salariya was born in Dundee, Scotland, where he studied illustration and printmaking. He has illustrated a wide range of books and has created many new series of books for publishers in the UK and overseas. In 1989 he established The Salariya Book Company. He lives in Brighton with his wife, the illustrator Shirley Willis, and their son.

U.S. Consultant:

Adam J. Mynarski

Author:

Ian Graham was born in Belfast in 1953. He studied applied physics at The City University, London, and took a postgraduate diploma in journalism at the same university, specializing in science and technology journalism. After four years as an editor of consumer electronics magazines, he became a freelance author and journalist. Since then, he has written more than one hundred children's non-fiction books and numerous magazine articles.

Artist:

Nick Hewetson was educated in Sussex at Brighton Technical School and studied illustration at Eastbourne College of Art. He has since illustrated a wide variety of children's books.

Editor:

Karen Barker Smith

Editorial Assistant:

Stephanie Cole

Created, designed, and produced by
THE SALARIYA BOOK COMPANY LTD
25 Marlborough Place, Brighton BN1 1UB

Repro by Modern Age

Reprinted in China in 2005

ISBN 0-531-14617-0 (Lib. Bdg.)
ISBN 0-531-14809-2 (Pbk.)

First American edition 2001 by Franklin Watts
Grolier Publishing Co.,Inc.
Sherman Turnpike
Danbury, CT 06816

Visit Franklin Watts on the Internet at:
http://publishing.grolier.com

A catalog record for this title is available from the Library of Congress.

SUPER
BIKES

Written by
IAN GRAHAM

Illustrated by
NICK HEWETSON

Created and designed by
DAVID SALARIYA

W
FRANKLIN WATTS
A Division of Grolier Publishing
NEW YORK • LONDON • HONG KONG • SYDNEY
DANBURY, CONNECTICUT

Contents

SUPER BIKES

The First Motorcycles

The first motorized bicycle (right) was built by the French Michaux brothers in 1869. They attached a steam engine to a bicycle frame.

In the 1880s and 1890s in Philadelphia, the Copeland brothers built steam-powered bicycles and tricycles (below). Bicycles were less popular than tricycles because the heavy steam engine made them difficult to balance.

The first bicycles powered by engines were built in the middle of the 19th century. Only steam engines could be used at that time, and they were far from ideal. Their fuel (coal or wood) was heavy and bulky and had to be burned for some time before the engine produced enough steam to move the vehicle. The engine was noisy and the burning fuel produced thick black smoke. Occasionally, steam engine boilers exploded! Gasoline engines, developed in the 1880s, were a great improvement. The moment the engine started, it could move the vehicle. The first motorcycles built for sale to the public, in the early 1900s, were pedal-powered bicycles with small engines added to them. By 1914, specially built motorcycles were being manufactured.

In the 1880s, the German engineers Gottlieb Daimler (below) and Wilhelm Maybach developed a small, high-speed internal-combustion engine suitable for powering vehicles. Instead of producing steam from water, it burned gasoline. In 1885, they attached the new engine to a wooden bicycle frame with stabilizer wheels at the sides. The engine turned the machine's rear wheel by means of a belt. The bike could manage a top speed of 12 mph (19 kph). Daimler went on to build cars, but he is still remembered as the inventor of the gasoline-engine motorcycle (right).

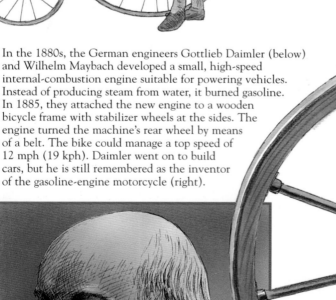

Daimler motorcycle

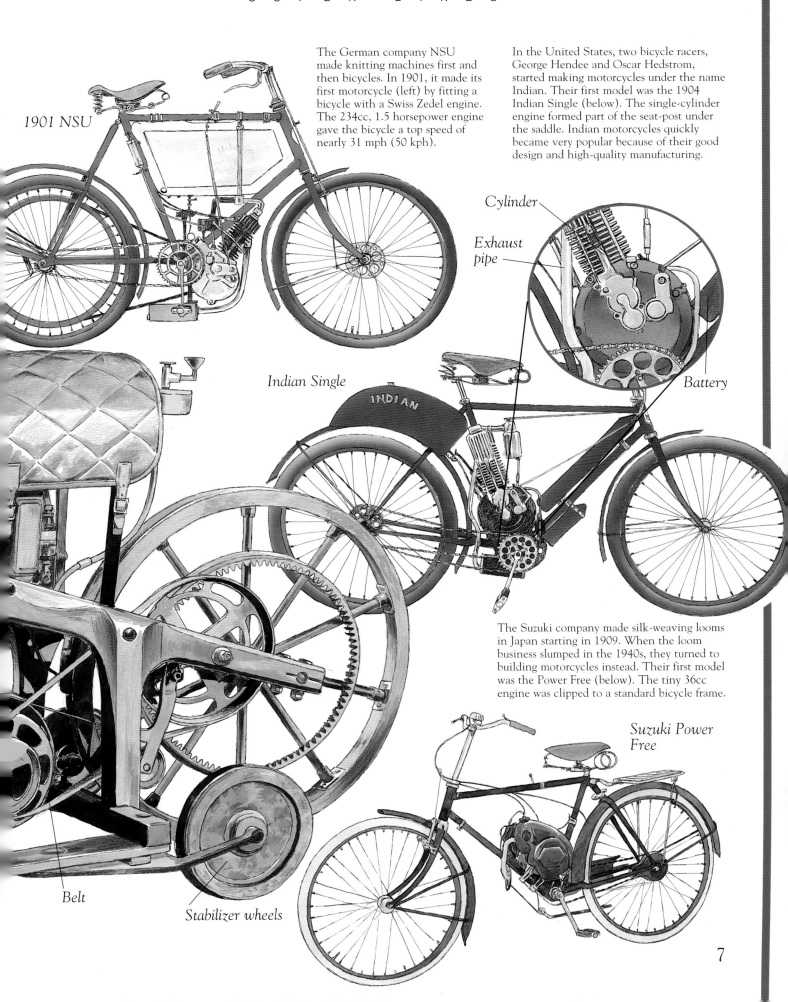

The German company NSU made knitting machines first and then bicycles. In 1901, it made its first motorcycle (left) by fitting a bicycle with a Swiss Zedel engine. The 234cc, 1.5 horsepower engine gave the bicycle a top speed of nearly 31 mph (50 kph).

In the United States, two bicycle racers, George Hendee and Oscar Hedstrom, started making motorcycles under the name Indian. Their first model was the 1904 Indian Single (below). The single-cylinder engine formed part of the seat-post under the saddle. Indian motorcycles quickly became very popular because of their good design and high-quality manufacturing.

1901 NSU

Cylinder

Exhaust pipe

Indian Single

INDIAN

Battery

The Suzuki company made silk-weaving looms in Japan starting in 1909. When the loom business slumped in the 1940s, they turned to building motorcycles instead. Their first model was the Power Free (below). The tiny 36cc engine was clipped to a standard bicycle frame.

Suzuki Power Free

Belt

Stabilizer wheels

The Grand Prix

The first Grand Prix race was a horse race that took place in France in 1863. As motorcycle racing grew in popularity in the early 1900s, it used the same name, Grand Prix, for its most important races. Grand Prix motorcycle races count toward an international championship. The most sought-after title in motorcycle racing is the 500cc Grand Prix world championship. There are Grand Prix classes for smaller 125cc and 250cc motorcycles. British motorcycles were the most successful in Grand Prix racing until the 1950s. Then Italian machines dominated the sport until the 1970s, when Japanese motorcycles took the lead.

John Surtees (left) set an amazing record in racing. He was one of the most successful motorcyclists of the late 1950s. After winning four 500cc and three 350cc world championships, he switched to car racing and reached the top in that sport as well, winning the 1964 Formula 1 championship. He later set up his own Formula 1 racing team. He is shown here sitting astride his 1956 MV Agusta Four. Its four-cylinder, 500cc engine gave it a top speed of 155 mph (250 kph).

A 1960s Grand Prix race

Modern racing tires are made from soft rubber, which grips the track best when it is warm. Before a race, the tires are heated by specially made electric blankets. These ensure that the riders can count on maximum grip from their tires.

Electric blankets

1970s

1980s

1990s

Sidecar racing (left) was at the height of its popularity in the 1950s-70s, when 500cc machines competed for the prestigious sidecar Grand Prix championship. Because of the sidecar, the rider cannot lean the motorcycle into a corner. If the rider corners too fast, the motorcycle rolls toward the outside of the corner. The passenger stops this by leaning into the corner.

The British motorcycle rider Barry Sheene (left) excelled in Grand Prix motorcycle racing in the 1970s. He won 24 Grand Prix races, earning him the 500cc world championship in 1976 and 1977.

Kenny Roberts (right) was the first American rider to win a world championship. He won the 500cc championship on his first attempt in 1978 and again in 1979 and 1980.

A 1990s Grand Prix race

Stunt Riders

Some people are not content to ride motorcycles in the normal way! Stunt riders use them to jump over things. Display teams pile people on top of them or ride them through fire. Motorcycle skiers hold on to the back of their bikes and slide along the ground behind them. Drag riders use specially designed motorcycles in one of the sport's fastest competition events. These stunts and extreme sports are highly dangerous. The teams of professionals who prepare the events and take part in them try to plan for every possibility, to make sure that everything works properly and that the riders go home in one piece. However, accidents do happen. The British stunt rider Eddie Kydd was very seriously injured when his motorcycle fell from an elevated landing ramp, ending his career. And the American stunt riders Evel and Robbie Knievel have both been injured while performing stunts.

Evel Knievel's son, Robbie (above), carried on in his father's footsteps as a sensational motorcycle stunt rider. His most spectacular feat was a jump over the Grand Canyon in 1999. His motorcycle soared off the takeoff ramp, sailed a record-breaking distance of 230 ft (70 m) through the air, and landed halfway down the landing ramp on the other side of the canyon. When the bike hit the rough desert floor, Knievel lost control and crashed, suffering two broken ribs and a sprained ankle.

Evel Knievel (above) is the world's best-known motorcycle stunt rider. His most famous jumps include a leap over 50 cars in the Los Angeles Coliseum. In 1974, he tried and failed to jump the Snake River Canyon in Idaho using a rocket-powered Harley-Davidson "skycycle." A parachute accidentally popped out on takeoff and he floated safely to the ground. His many crash landings are said to have broken nearly every bone in his body!

A motorcycle stunt rider soars off the takeoff ramp in a spectacular jump (left).

Two drag riders prepare to accelerate like rockets down the straight drag strip. Small wheels at the rear of the bikes stop them from rearing up as the engines roar into life.

Until the 1960s, organizations that used motorcycles, such as police forces, often had their own display teams that toured the country. Outdoor events frequently featured displays by these teams. The riders criss-crossed an arena in a complex display of precision riding skills. The stunts they performed for the crowds included carrying a pyramid of people on top of a line of motorcycles (left) and jumping motorcycles over obstacles, through hoops, and through fire (right).

In one of the most unusual and dangerous motorcycle stunts, motorcycle skiing (above), a bike accelerates to top speed, then the rider slips backward over the seat and steps onto the track! With showers of sparks flying from his steel-soled boots, he holds on to the back of his bike. In 1999, the record was set at an incredible speed of 156 mph (251 kph) by British rider Gary Rothwell, using a Suzuki Hayabusa.

Angelle Seeling (right) is one of only a handful of women to compete in motorcycle drag racing. The former intensive care nurse from Louisiana began racing drag bikes in 1996.

ACEWAY

Motorcycle racers often celebrate winning by doing a wheelie (above). In 1999, the world record for the fastest wheelie was set at 191 mph (307 kph) by Swedish rider Patrik Furstenhoff on a Honda Blackbird.

15

The Yamaha YZF-R1 outperforms most comparable sports motorcycles. The key to its sizzling performance on the road is its engine power and light weight. The YZF-R1's designers looked at every part of the motorcycle and investigated ways to make it lighter. As a result of their work, the whole machine weighs only 390 lb (177 kg).

The YZF-R1's silencer, attached to the engine exhaust pipe to reduce engine noise, is made from titanium, a lightweight and corrosion-resistant metal. Its handlebars are bonded (glued) in place instead of welded, to save weight. By using a new type of plastic, the bodywork was made 25% thinner and therefore lighter than normal motorbikes. The metal wheels have thinner walls than usual and they have only three spokes. The disc brakes on the front and rear wheels have been slimmed down by 2/100 in (.5 mm) to save a few more ounces. Even the instruments the rider looks at have been made lighter. The bike's four-cylinder engine is also smaller and lighter than most comparable engines. It weighs only 143 lb (65 kg), but it achieves 150 bhp (brake horse-power) — that's more powerful than some small European cars up to seven times the weight of the YZF-R1. It can achieve a top speed of 174 mph (280 kph).

Ducati 996

Fuel tank

Engine

Silencer

Rear view of the Yamaha YZF-R1

Disc brake

Front view of the Yamaha YZF-R1

Yamaha YZF-R1

The Italian motorcycle manufacturer Ducati is famous for its racing motorcycles. Ducatis, in the capable hands of British rider Carl Fogarty, have won four Superbike world championships. Ducati also makes highly desirable road machines such as the 996 (left). Its 996cc engine, lightweight tubular frame, and streamlined shape give it a top speed of 162 mph (260 kph).

Handlebars

Spoke

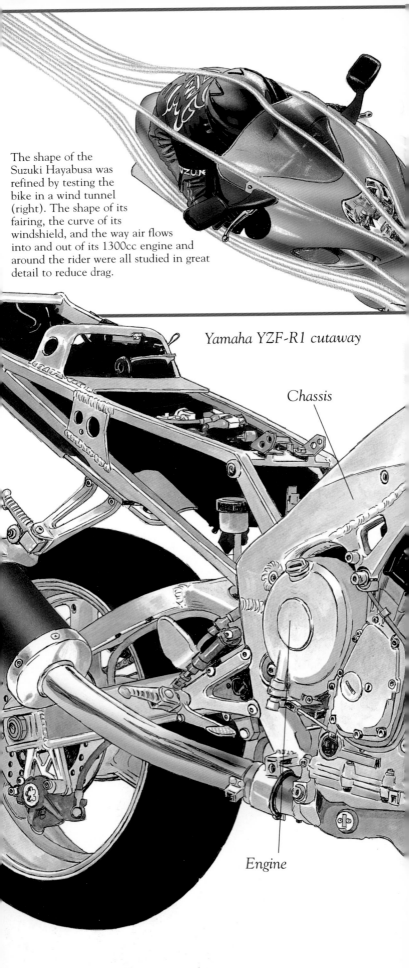

The shape of the Suzuki Hayabusa was refined by testing the bike in a wind tunnel (right). The shape of its fairing, the curve of its windshield, and the way air flows into and out of its 1300cc engine and around the rider were all studied in great detail to reduce drag.

Yamaha YZF-R1 cutaway

Chassis

Engine

Suzuki Hayabusa

The Suzuki Hayabusa (above) is the world's fastest production motorcycle. It can reach an amazing top speed of 186 mph (300 kph). It was named Hayabusa after a Japanese falcon that can also cut through the air at this speed.

Radiator

High Performance

High-performance sports road bikes are built to look like racing machines. Their sporty performance is produced by a combination of engine power, a smooth shape, and light weight. Small sports motorcycles have engines with two cylinders, while the biggest machines have four-cylinder engines. If two cylinders are set at an angle to each other, forming a V shape, the engine is called a V-twin. A smooth cover called a fairing hides most of the engine and makes the bike more streamlined. The heavier any vehicle is, the more engine power it needs. Every ounce saved improves a motorcycle's performance, so sports bike designers put a great deal of effort into saving weight wherever possible.

Suzuki TL1000R

The Suzuki TL1000R (above) is a sleek, streamlined machine. Its big 1,000cc V-twin engine gives it a top speed of more than 150 mph (240 kph).

Honda's Fireblade (below) is a super all-around sports bike with a winning blend of power, speed, and balance. Its 900cc four-cylinder engine gives a top speed of 165 mph (265 kph).

Honda Fireblade

Cal Rayborn (below) won the Daytona 200 race in Florida in 1968 and 1969. In 1970 he set a motorcycle land speed record of 265 mph (427 kph). His sparkling career was cut short when he was killed while racing in New Zealand in 1973.

Cal Rayborn

In endurance races, motorcycles have to visit the pits from time to time to be refueled and have their tires changed (below). During these pit stops, which usually take only a few seconds, riders often change over too. Fast pit stops are essential because a race lasting several hours can be won or lost by just a fraction of a second.

Super Stars

Motorcycle sports test riders and their machines in many different ways. Long-distance endurance races last for up to 24 hours. The most famous include the 24-hour Le Mans race in France and the Suzuka 8-hour race in Japan. Teams of two or three riders take turns to keep each motorcycle on the track for the whole race without a break. Road races, such as the Tourist Trophy races held on the Isle of Man, challenge riders to compete at high speeds on normal roads with bumps, bends, curbs, and roadside signs. One form of motorcycle sport, superbike racing, has become hugely popular in recent years. It began in the United States in the 1970s, using modified road bikes. Some of the most successful Grand Prix motorcyclists started racing on superbikes.

Carl Fogarty (left) is one of the most successful riders in motorcycling but he has never competed in Grand Prix races. He is a champion superbike rider. Superbike riders compete on motorcycles that are very similar to road bikes (below). Few modifications to the bikes are allowed, so the races are close. Nowadays, superbike racing rivals Grand Prix racing for popularity and excitement.

Refueling

Superbike rider

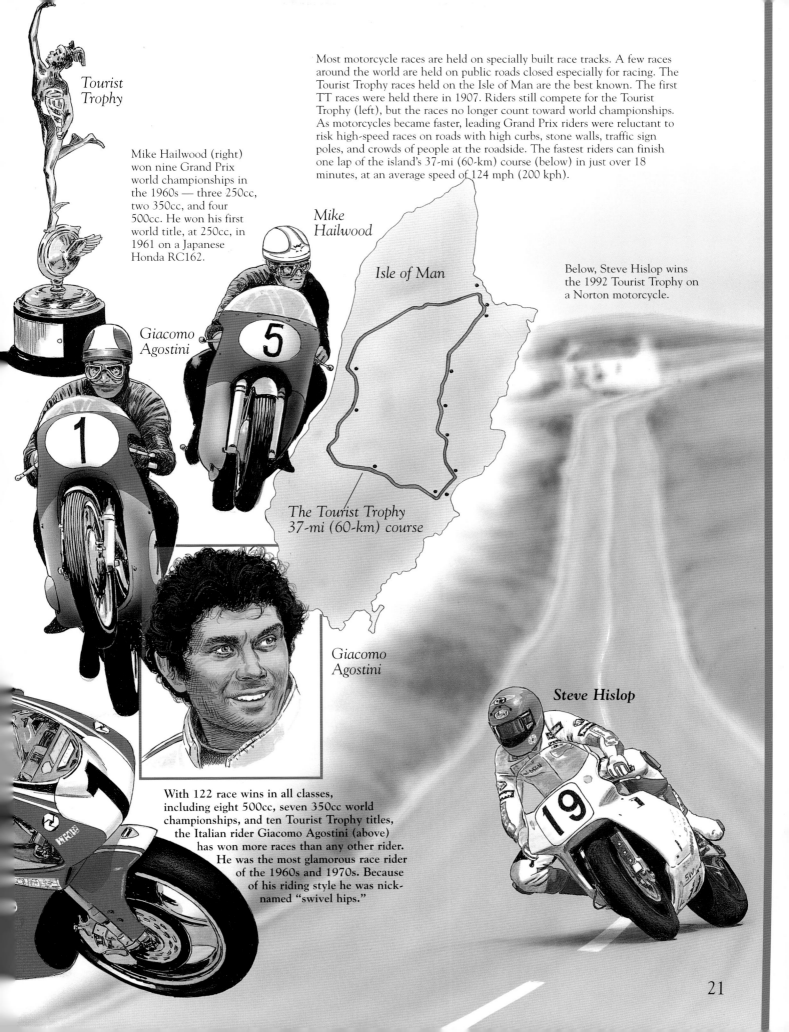

Tourist Trophy

Mike Hailwood (right) won nine Grand Prix world championships in the 1960s — three 250cc, two 350cc, and four 500cc. He won his first world title, at 250cc, in 1961 on a Japanese Honda RC162.

Mike Hailwood

Giacomo Agostini

Most motorcycle races are held on specially built race tracks. A few races around the world are held on public roads closed especially for racing. The Tourist Trophy races held on the Isle of Man are the best known. The first TT races were held there in 1907. Riders still compete for the Tourist Trophy (left), but the races no longer count toward world championships. As motorcycles became faster, leading Grand Prix riders were reluctant to risk high-speed races on roads with high curbs, stone walls, traffic sign poles, and crowds of people at the roadside. The fastest riders can finish one lap of the island's 37-mi (60-km) course (below) in just over 18 minutes, at an average speed of 124 mph (200 kph).

Isle of Man

Below, Steve Hislop wins the 1992 Tourist Trophy on a Norton motorcycle.

The Tourist Trophy 37-mi (60-km) course

Giacomo Agostini

With 122 race wins in all classes, including eight 500cc, seven 350cc world championships, and ten Tourist Trophy titles, the Italian rider Giacomo Agostini (above) has won more races than any other rider. He was the most glamorous race rider of the 1960s and 1970s. Because of his riding style he was nick-named "swivel hips."

Steve Hislop

Dirt Devils

Motorcycles are raced on every type of surface. Loose surfaces like sand, dirt, and shale are difficult to race on because motorcycle tires can't grip them well. When riders lean their bikes over to go around corners, they have to put a foot down to stop the bikes from falling over. One of the most popular loose surface sports is supercross, or motocross, which involves racing around a bumpy, muddy course. Speedway events are races held on very slippery oval-shaped tracks made from dirt or shale. Races are also held on the slipperiest surface of all — ice. There are even races through deserts.

Motocross rider

Motocross bike

A motocross bike (above) has very springy wheels that can bounce up and down a long way. This helps keep the bike level across bumpy ground. Speedway bikes (left) are light and low and have no brakes. They burn methanol instead of gasoline, which is held in a tiny 1/2-gallon (2-liter) tank. Top speed is less important than fast acceleration — a speedway bike can go from a standing start to 60 mph (95 kph) in two seconds. Desert bikes (far left) are completely different. They are bigger and much heavier — perhaps four times the weight of a speedway bike. They are also higher off the ground to cope with rough terrain, and they have a bigger fuel tank.

Desert bike

Speedway bike

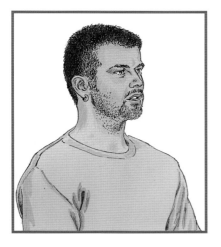

The U.S. rider Jeremy McGrath (left) started racing bikes when he was 5 years old. Since then he has won the 1995 AMA 250cc National Motocross Championship, the 1994 and 1995 FIM World Supercross Championships, and the AMA 250cc Supercross Championships in 1993, 1994, 1995, 1996, 1998, and 1999.

Desert racing

Motorcycle trials are completely different. They involve riding over large obstacles such as rocks and tree trunks. Unlike in other loose surface sports, in trials, riders are not allowed to put a foot down to steady themselves. Regulations control the bike design for these various events, so that they are evenly matched and the races are close and exciting.

The world's most famous desert race is the Paris-Dakar rally, in which riders cross the Sahara Desert in North Africa. It can be difficult to find the right route in the desert, and getting lost is dangerous. In long desert races, groups of riders often stay within sight of each other for safety.

Ice racing is popular in some countries. Ice-racing motorcycles have tires covered in steel spikes (below). The sharp spikes are vital to help the tires grip the ice, especially when the riders lean their bikes to the side to take a corner.

The fastest way to go around a bend in a speedway race is to lean the bike over and let the rear wheel swing right out to the side (below). The rider puts one steel-soled boot down and slides it along the ground to stop the bike from falling over.

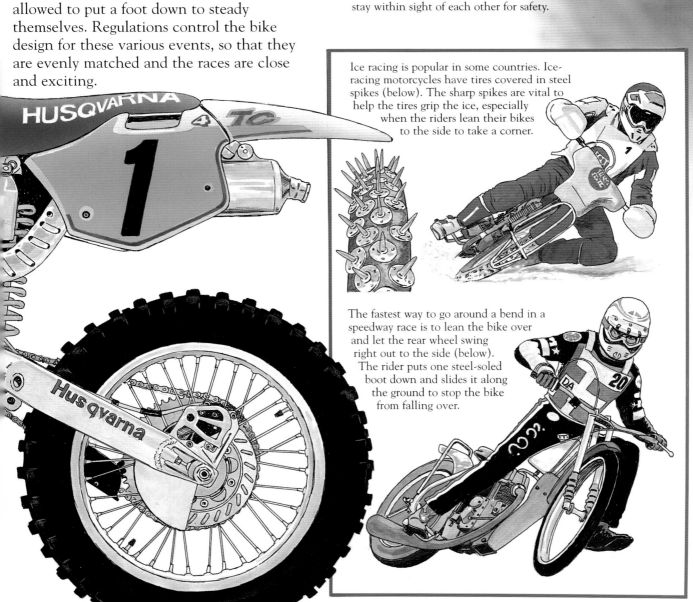

Honda X-Wing

Some future motorcycles will combine the advanced engineering and design of today's motorcycles with the safety and comfort of today's scooters. The 1500cc Honda X-Wing (above) is a prototype of one of these future "super-scooters."

Some designers have produced very dramatic versions of what they think future motorcycles might look like. This stunning dream bike (right) is based on a real motorcycle, the 1000cc Suzuki TL1000S sports road bike.

Bikes to Come

Motorcycle design is always developing. By using metals such as aluminum and new materials such as carbon fiber, bikes can be made to weigh less, which means they use less power. Because of this they burn less fuel, which is kinder to the environment. More efficient engines further reduce the amount of fuel burned. The shape of a motorcycle must be practical — there has to be enough space for the engine, fuel tank, and other parts. Faster sports bikes have a streamlined fairing to cut air resistance. However, motorcycles are not just practical vehicles. Their appearance changes with changing fashions, new ideas from designers, the popularity of certain motorcycle sports, and even the types of motorcycles that appear in films.

A futuristic bike design based on the Suzuki TL1000S

Aprilia's Moto 6.5 roadster (below) looks very different from its usual style of road-going models. The Italian manufacturer Aprilia is well known for its racing motorcycles and road-going sports motorcycles. Technical advances and engineering developments on the racetrack are used to improve the design and performance of its road bikes. The Moto 6.5 roadster was created for Aprilia by the French designer Philippe Starck. His aim was to combine the most advanced technology with a timeless look that would not date.

Aprilia Moto 6.5

Harley-Davidson

Harley-Davidson

Motorcycles have grown bigger over the years, but they will never equal the biggest Harley-Davidson in the world (above). It was built by the owner of a motorcycle shop in California. The "rider" sits inside the five-ton machine which is 46 ft (14 m) long and stands 26 ft (8 m) high. Its 5-liter Cadillac car engine gives it a top speed of 80 mph (130 kph).

The latest motorcycles are not always sleek and streamlined machines. New bikes that look as if they were made long ago are popular, too (left). It's called retro styling. So, some motorcycles of the future may copy the designs of today's machines.

25

Racing clothing

Racing motorcyclists wear full-face helmets to protect their whole head, face, and jaw. Slots let air flow through the helmet, to keep the rider's head cool and to stop the visor from misting up.

Visor

Extra pieces of body armor are sometimes worn underneath the leather outer suit to give added protection to areas such as the hips.

Thick pads called sliders protect the rider's knees, which often touch the ground on corners.

Slider

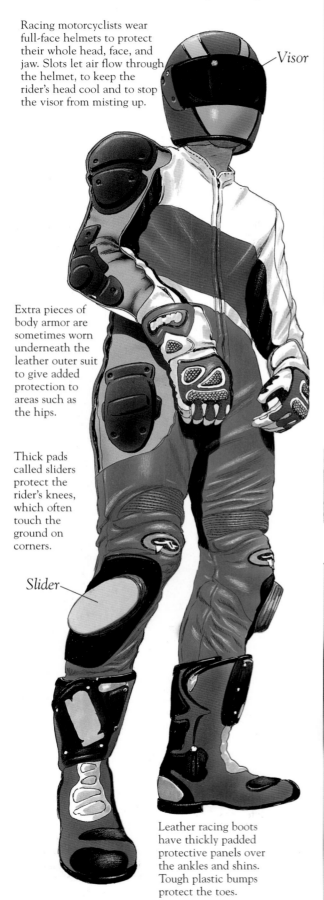

Leather racing boots have thickly padded protective panels over the ankles and shins. Tough plastic bumps protect the toes.

Bike Safety

It is vital that motorcyclists protect themselves from injury by wearing the right clothing. Head protection is especially important. A motorcycle helmet works in two ways to prevent brain damage. Its hard outer shell stops the skull from being fractured or crushed, while its soft lining cushions it. Clothing protects the rest of the body from scrapes and cuts. The clothing is thicker and tougher over easily damaged areas of the body such as the knees, elbows, and the backs of the hands. Leather is a favorite material for motorcycle clothing because when scraped along the ground, it wears away without tearing. Tough plastic spine protectors are sometimes worn inside the clothes to give added back protection.

Racing motorcyclists take their machines to the limit (right). A momentary loss of tire grip can upset the delicate balance of the bike, especially when cornering. It can make a bike slide out of a corner and spill the rider onto the track. Racing motorcyclists wear all-in-one suits called leathers. Leathers give a rider's body a smooth outline to cut drag and to provide some skin protection if the rider comes off the bike and slides along the track. Even so, riders can suffer burns from friction between the track and their leathers.

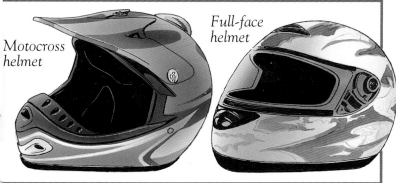

Motocross helmet

Full-face helmet

Full-face helmet

Tear-resistant jacket

Leather gloves

Armored jeans

Motorcycle boots are made in different styles. Many riders like the classic black leather boot, while others prefer the more casual desert boot. They support the toes and ankles. Some protect the shins, too.

Some motorcycle safety clothing is made to look more like normal casual clothes. Armored jeans, for example, have tough pads sewn into the material to protect the rider in case of an accident.

Glossary

Aluminum
A light, silver-colored metal.

Brake horsepower (bhp)
A measurement of engine power.

Carbon fiber
A solid, strong, and light material that can withstand high temperatures. It is used to make motorcyclists' safety clothing.

Combustion
Another word for "burning."

Cylinder
One of the tube-shaped chambers in an engine where fuel is burned.

Disc brakes
Brakes that work by using pads to grip a steel disc on the wheel.

Drag
Air resistance; air pushing against a motorcycle slows it down.

Dragster
An immensely powerful motorcycle used for drag racing.

Fairing
A streamlined covering that wraps around the engine of a motorcycle to make the bike slip through the air more easily.

Fuel
A liquid such as gasoline that is changed to a vapor and burned inside an engine.

Horsepower
A measure of how fast an engine converts the energy in its fuel into movement energy.

Internal-combustion engine
A type of engine that burns fuel inside the engine.

Kevlar
A tough man-made material used in clothing for motorcyclists. It is five times stronger than the same weight of steel.

Pits
Garages at the side of racetracks where bikes can be refueled and riders changed.

Prototype
A model of a bike, used to test the design before the bike goes into production.

Scooter
A light motorcycle with a footboard for resting the feet on between the engine and front wheel.

Shale
A surface of fine gravely rock.

Silencer
A pipe-shaped chamber attached to a motorcycle engine's exhaust pipe to reduce engine noise.

Titanium
An extremely tough yet lightweight metal that does not corrode and can withstand very high temperatures.

Tubular frame
A motorcycle frame made from metal tubes welded together.

Welded
Pieces of metal joined together by heating.

Super Bikes Facts

The size of a motorcycle engine — 250cc for example — is the size of the cylinders inside the engine, where the fuel is burned.

The badge of the Japanese motorcycle manufacturer, Yamaha, shows three tuning forks because the company originally made musical instruments.

Racing bikes use tires without any tread, called slicks. They can only be used on a dry track. In wet weather, tires with tread, called wets, are used.

The lap record at the Isle of Man TT race is held by Superbike champion Carl Fogarty. In 1992, he set the fastest ever average lap speed of 122 mph (197 kph).

John Surtees is the only person to win Grand Prix championships on both two and four wheels.

Racing motorcyclists lean over so far when they are cornering that the knee on the inside of the bend slides along the ground.

The U.S. racing motorcyclist Dave Aldana wore a leather racing suit in the early 1970s with a skeleton painted on it.

Not all motorcycles have two wheels! Four-wheeled motorcycles called quad bikes are used for sport, recreation, and farming. Farmers use them to get around land more quickly than on foot and to help round up animals.

On a fast lap, the rear tire of a racing bike gets hotter than boiling water. Temperatures around 257°F (125°C) are common.

Since the beginning of the motorcycle industry, more than 2,000 different makes of motorbikes have been produced.

The first specially built motor racetrack in the world was laid at Brooklands in Surrey, England. It was closed in 1938.

In 1923 the American E.J. Christie designed a large single-wheeled motorbike, which he claimed would reach a speed of 248 mph (400 kph). However, there is no evidence that his machine was a success.

Chronology

1869 The French Michaux brothers add a small steam engine to a bicycle and build the first motorized two-wheeled vehicle.

1885 Gottlieb Daimler and Wilhelm Maybach build the first gasoline engine motorcycle.

1888 John Boyd Dunlop invents the pneumatic (air-filled) tire.

1894 The first mass-produced motorcycle is manufactured by Heinrich Hildebrand and Alois Wolfmüller.

1899 The first military motorcycle is built for service in the Boer War. A Maxim machine-gun is attached to a French de Dion motorized tricycle.

1902 The first motor scooter is built in France. It is called an Autofauteuil, which means "motor-armchair"!

1904 The first Harley-Davidson motorcycle, called the Silent Gray Fellow, is manufactured in the United States.

1906 Motorcycle racing begins on the Isle of Man.

1907 The first Tourist Trophy motorcycle race is held on the Isle of Man.

1909 The first motorcycle speed record, 76 mph (122 kph), is set by William Cook at the Brooklands racetrack in England.

1910 The sidecar is invented.

1911 The Mountain Course is used for the first time for the Isle of Man Tourist Trophy motorcycle race. It is still used today.

1912 Carl Stevens Clancy becomes the first person to ride a motorcycle around the world.

1913 The first motorcycle with an electric starter motor, the Indian Hendee Special, is

manufactured, but electric starter motors do not become commonplace until the 1960s.

1914 Motorcycles are fitted with machine guns for use in World War I. Other motorcycles are fitted with sidecars and used as ambulances.

1915 The American company Indian becomes the biggest motorcycle manufacturer in the world.

1920 The first official motorcycle land speed record, 104 mph (167 kph), is set by Ernie Walker on an Indian motorcycle at Daytona Beach, Florida.

1937 A Harley-Davidson model 61 ridden by Joe Petrali sets an ocean-level land speed record for motorcycles of 136 mph (219 kph).

1939 The first motorcycles designed specifically as military motorcycles are built for use in World War II.

1958 A standard specification for motorcycle helmets is developed in the United States after the death of an amateur rider, Peter Snell, because of poor helmet design.

1960 John Surtees wins the last of his four 500cc and three 350cc Grand Prix championships.

1961 Mike Hailwood wins the 250cc Grand Prix championship, the first of three 250cc, two 350cc, and four 500cc world titles.

1966 Bob Leppan sets a new motorcycle land speed record of 245 mph (395 kph).

1970 U.S. motorcyclist Cal Rayborn sets a new motorcycle land speed record of 265 mph (427 kph).

1973 Cal Rayborn is killed while racing in New Zealand.

1974 U.S. stunt rider Evel Knievel's attempt to jump his rocket-powered motorcycle over the Snake River Canyon in Idaho fails when a parachute opens too early.

1975 Italian motorcycle racer Giacomo Agostini wins the 500cc Grand Prix championship, the last of his eight 500cc and seven 350cc titles.

1978 Donald Vesco sets a motorcycle land speed record of 318 mph (512 kph) on his Lightning Bolt motorcycle, a specially built machine powered by two Kawasaki motorcycle engines.

1979 The first Paris-Dakar rally is held.

1980 Kenny Roberts wins the last of his three consecutive 500cc Grand Prix championships.

1981 U.S. stunt rider Evel Knievel retires.

1983 The first rocket-propelled motorcycle is built by Dutch drag racer Henk Vink. It can reach a top speed of 248 mph (400 kph).

1989 The first World Superbike Championship is held. It is won by Fred Merkel on a Honda.

1990 Dave Campos, riding a Harley-Davidson powered machine, sets a new motorcycle land speed record of 322 mph (518 kph).

1994 Mike Doohan wins the first of his five 500cc Grand Prix championships.

1999 U.S. stunt rider Robbie Knievel jumps his motorcycle over the Grand Canyon in Arizona.

2000 Robbie Knievel jumps his motorcycle over a moving railway locomotive.

Index

Illustrations are shown in **bold** type.